Cover Page

Little Glimpses of the Eternal, Book 1
--- Seeking the Unknowable

Book 1 - Messages from My Heart

Moses at the Burning Bush

Jim Leonard

Title Page

Little Glimpses of the Eternal, Bk 1 --- Seeking the Unknowable

Book 1 - Messages from My Heart

Jim Leonard

Copyright Page

Published by Dac Says Publishing,
San Luis Obispo, CA, 93401

To contact Publisher or Author, email:
jamesleonard08@gmail.com

Front and back cover design by Cover
Creator, CreateSpace.com

Free front cover image by:
www.workersforjesus.com

Printed in the United States of America

Copyright Page continued

First Printing 2016

ISBN 10: 0-9884076-5-5
ISBN 13: 978-0-9884076-5-7

Dedication

To: My youngest daughter, Angela (2 April 2016).

You are the one person in my life that continually pulls at my heartstrings. Even today, you are helping me to stay focused on the endgame, namely, finding the very center of my soul. You have shaped my spiritual (and worldly) path. Thank you for guiding and enhancing my journey.

Foreword

This book is an attempt to document my spiritual (and worldly) life, mainly after The 911 Event. Immediately after that event, I lost my consulting position with a software development firm, lost my home in Arlington, TX, entered into bankruptcy, and had to decide between moving to the East Coast (Brooklyn, NY) or West Coast (Santa Ana or San Luis Obispo, CA). I chose west, near my youngest daughter's family.

I also decided to write this book in autobiographical form, using my events in a Roman Catholic Church (RCC) rather than ordering it entirely with the Calendar. The location and event are the greatest significance for my spiritual (and worldly) path. Some events were epiphanies in my spiritual formation and growth. Further, most of the events were little glimpses of the eternal for me. And I believe they were messages directly from my heart.

Table of Contents

1. Communication from Above

On-line dictionaries define a glimpse as a very brief, passing look, sight, or view; a momentary or slight appearance; or a vague idea; inkling. Further synonyms for the word glimpse include perceive, notice, detect, spot, catch sight of; all catching sight of communication from above; namely, from the Immortal One, the Eternal One, our Heavenly Father, or God himself.

The image of Moses at the Burning Bush on the cover of this book has special significance for me. It symbolizes my posture during meditative prayers, namely, approaching God as a humble creature with reverence and awe.

The communication events in this book are about glimpsing, seeking, and striving for spiritual union with the Almighty Creator of heaven and earth. At times I get some indication that my prayers are being answered but usually in a totally unexpected and surprising way. Other times, when praying for discernment of a particular goal, I find a hint of things to come or confirmation of a selected path. It feels good to know I am being guided. There is also a comfort knowing I am on the right track.

It is through these communications from above that I believe our Heavenly Father, the Almighty Creator of heaven and earth, is letting me know the source of ideas that flash through my mind. I believe the Creator enabled me to know the source of particular ideas. I am convinced that they came from my own heart, namely *Messages from My Own Heart.* The following locations and events are examples of these brief and fleeting glimpses of the eternal for me.

1.1 Parish Churches and Cathedrals

Parish churches and cathedrals in the RCC serve their respective communities throughout the world. Some of the Catholic terminology used in this book includes:
- **Catholic**: Relating to the RCC.
- **Cathedral**: The central church of diocese (many parishes) that serves as the chair (authority) of its bishop.
- **Communion**: A priest says the words of Jesus (this is my body, and this is my blood) over bread and wine (the elements of Holy Communion) and then shares communion with the worshippers.
- **Eucharist:** The consecrated elements of Holy Communion (bread and wine).
- **Gospel**: The heart of the sacred books for Christians because they are the principal source of the life and teachings of Jesus Christ. The term gospel refers to any of the first four books of the New Testament, namely Matthew, Mark, Luke, and John.
- **Liturgy**: The common formulas for the conduct of the divine services in Christian churches.
- **Mass**: The celebration of the Eucharist that commemorates the death of Jesus. A High Mass is celebrated according to the full rite (the liturgy is sung). In a Low Mass, the liturgy is spoken not sung.
- **RCC**: Roman Catholic Church.
- **RCIA**: The process of reconciling an adult

2

into full communion with the RCC.

- **Vatican II**: The 2nd Vatican Ecumenical Council (1962 - 1965) of the RCC. Redefined the nature of the church. Increased lay participation in the liturgy.

As a result of Vatican II, priests celebrate Mass (using their native language), face the congregation, and signal worshippers that they are a vital component of the Mass.

- **Baptism**: Regeneration of a person, through water and the Word of God.
- **Confirmation:** Seals a person with the gift of the Holy Spirit.
- **Minister**: Person authorized by the RCC to perform various functions in the church.
- **Priest**: An ordained male member of the clergy below that of a bishop, and permitted to carry out the Christian ministry.
- **Sacrament**: Baptism, penance, confirmation, the Eucharist, holy orders, matrimony, and anointing of the sick.

1.1.1 Sacred Heart Church, Prescott, AZ

I was raised Catholic, baptized, confirmed, and married in RCCs. I divorced in 1976 and subsequently fell away from the church. My youngest daughter (born in 1965) drew me back into the church by wanting me to receive Holy Communion during her *Confirmation* ceremony.

In 1987, I was working in Prescott, AZ, so I found the Sacred Heart Catholic Church, completed their RCIA program, and became reconciled with the church. The RCIA helped me to get familiar with post-Vatican II (after 1962) Catholic Church, and I liked it.

My RCIA instruction and reconciliation required participation in eight weekly two-hour sessions with fifteen individuals. Toward the end of the sessions, I became fascinated with the "New" Church and I began sensing guidance from above. It was an exciting time for me, back to the church, and resolution of an early failure in my spiritual life (and that of my youngest daughter). This was a little glimpse of the eternal for me.

1.1.2 St. Vincent de Paul Church, San Diego, CA

At my daughter's birth in 1965, she was not baptized, and this fact was always on my mind and became a deep concern. In 1985 she found a deacon and received religious instruction at St. Vincent de Paul RCC in San Diego, CA.

Then she asked if I would join her for Holy Communion at her *Confirmation Mass*. My answer was "Yes, anywhere, anytime." She wanted to make sure that I fully understood the commitment, explaining that I needed to be reconciled with the Church to receive Holy Communion.

I responded, "I understand, and I will do it. Let me know the date and time of the confirmation. I am very happy about you taking these steps on your own."

In the spring of 1987, I attended the *Confirmation Mass* and happily received my daughter in full communion with the Church.

4

This step was a new beginning for her and me. The Holy Spirit put us both on this path. And I was learning to see with the eyes of my heart. It was another little glimpse of the eternal for me.

1.1.3 Holy Family Cathedral, Orange, CA

In November of 2013, I was in the hospital (St. Joseph Hospital, Orange, CA) for a few days with an irregular heart cycle. Each morning I received Holy Communion from local parish ministers. One day the minister was from my parish, but I did not know her. I asked, "What Mass do you attend"? She answered at 8:15 am. Following my release from the hospital, I wanted to thank her for visiting me. The 8:15 am *Mass*, however, was not good for me.

Then on January 1st, 2014 there was only one *Mass* for the day (9 am), the Solemnity of Mary. I arrived early and sat near the place where I used to take my mother. A woman dressed in red sat down near me. As she moved to the aisle to distribute Holy Communion, I recognized her.

After communion, I touched her left hand and said, "I finally get a chance to thank you for bringing me communion at the hospital." She gave me a puzzled look. "Around Halloween at St. Joseph's Hospital." She smiled but didn't remember me. At the instant I saw her, I knew in my heart that it was not a coincidence, nearly 800 people at *Mass*, and she sat down right next to me. It was a little glimpse of the eternal.

Eucharistic Ministers for the homebound or hospital-bound are spreading the Gospel (good news) of Jesus Christ, by their example of kindness and compassion to those in need. These trained individuals distribute Holy Communion, engage in prayer, and read the appropriate *Gospel* for the day. These acts extend the spiritual (and worldly) community for those unable to attend *Mass*.

1.1.4 St. Raphael's RCC, Kauai, HI

My trip to Kauai (November 25th, through December 2nd, 2014) included: Thanksgiving dinner near Poipu (south side of the island) with my eldest daughter and son-in-law, and Sunday *Mass* at the St. Raphael Catholic Church.

On Saturday, November 30th, my daughter, and son-in-law helped me find the church. It was located beyond the old church (under renovation). Upon entering the new church, I saw a woman standing near the altar, directing others in preparation for Sunday's 11 am *Mass*. I asked her about the seating on Sunday and a good place for a visitor to sit. She pointed to the pews directly in front of the lectern saying, "always plenty of seating in this section of the church."

The next day, I entered the church at 10:45 am and went to the area the woman suggested. I looked around and noticed the same woman was at the lectern leading the congregation in the *Holy Rosary*. The *Rosary* is a prayer of devotion to God by meditating

6

on the lives of Jesus and Mary.

The woman was reading a *Scripture* passage, and then while waiting for the response, she looked up and then directly at me and smiled. I joined in praying the *Rosary,* and it was a splendid preparation for *Mass*.

After *Mass*, I walked over to the old church and took a few photos. I thought about getting a few souvenirs; found the gift shop, picked out a journal, a small book about St. Raphael (the Archangel), and two prayer cards. The cashier was the same woman, and she was only taking cash, no credit cards. I explained my situation to her: no money, but my daughter was picking me up in a few minutes and asked her to hold them for me. She agreed.

When my daughter arrived with some cash, I rushed back to find the gift shop had closed. Then, I walked to the front office; the same woman came out with my package, and we finished the transaction. I am quite sure St. Raphael interceded on my behalf, which made my experience enjoyable and memorable. Another little glimpse of the eternal for me.

Volunteers at parish churches provide great assistance in spreading the *Gospel* message to parishioners and visitors. They also respond to every opportunity to participate in the *Mass*. The volunteers serve as Eucharistic ministers, altar servers, lectors (readers of *Scripture*), collection servers, or greeters. All of these positions help the parish community, and more importantly; they enable an increase in the volunteers' personal knowledge of the *Mass* and thereby open avenues for their spiritual growth.

1.1.5 St. Norbert's RCC, Orange, CA

On May 2nd, 2014 my oldest daughter drove me to St. Norbert's Catholic Church. I wanted to make a confession (disclosure of sin or sinfulness, especially to a priest to obtain absolution) however; the parish priests were out of town on their annual retreat. While in the church, I said a few prayers and had a very good feeling about the church.

Then we drove about 4 miles to the Holy Family Cathedral in Orange, CA and found a similar note "Only an 8:15 am Mass today, as the priests are on retreat."

The drive was good as we joked about a few things while I saw some of my original driving routes in Santa Ana, Orange, and Villa Park, CA. She was helping me to continue my spiritual (and worldly) journey, and this was possibly another little glimpse of the eternal for me. Although this attempt to make a confession failed, a few weeks later my daughter and son-in-law helped me to succeed.

I prepared an examination of my conscience and confessed my sins to the priest. Then I said an act of contrition (detestation of past sins and a resolve to make amends) and received absolution (forgiveness) and penance (prayer of fasting as a voluntary self-punishment to atone for sins) from the priest.

Check on-line at the National Catholic Register for a simple guide for confession for adults, including an examination of conscience, and prayers to say before and after confession.

1.1.6 St. Philip Benizi RCC, Fullerton, CA

This RCC served as my parish community for two years following my move to Fullerton, CA (spring of 2011). During this time I became a regular communicant at the 8:30 am *Mass*, on weekdays and Sunday.

I encountered the Scriptural Rosary at this parish and found it much easier for me to stay focused on the theme of each decade of the Rosary. Some of the church regulars had breakfast together following Mass. For a few days my brother, Larry joined us. He was traveling to CA from his home in Wyoming. During my time at this parish, I met with Father David for counseling and spiritual direction and found the sessions to be insightful and helpful. And they provided another little glimpse of the eternal for me.

Throughout this time I felt called to do more at church. I tried to become a lector, a reader of *Scripture during Mass*, but it didn't work out. Then medical problems required moving to Santa Ana, CA and I became a parishioner of the Holy Family Cathedral in Orange, CA.

1.1.7 Sacred Heart Church, Greybull, WY

This RCC located in Greybull, WY was the site of a *Sunday Mass* and *Anointing of the*

Sick in 2010. The celebration included: *Sunday Mass (The Word and the Eucharist)* followed by *Anointing of the Sick*, where the priest lays hands on the sick; prays over them, then anoints them with oil blessed by the bishop.

My brother and I were traveling from Pinedale, WY, south to Riverton, around the southern end of the Wind River Mountain Range, north to Greybull (spend the night), and then directly west to an entrance of Yellowstone National Park. It was a happy time for us, and the receipt of these blessings was an unexpected gift, possibly another little glimpse of the eternal.

1.1.8 Nativity of Our Lady Church SLO, CA

At this RCC, located in San Luis Obispo, CA, I was involved in many charity group meetings, *Bible studies*, ordinations, funerals, and other Catholic celebrations. The *Bible studies* provided several opportunities for spiritual growth. I experienced several little glimpses of the eternal.

- **The *Bible*** *(God's Word)* consists of the sacred books of the *Old and New Testaments*.
- **Ordination** in the RCC is the process by which male deacons and priests are consecrated (set apart) as clergy, for various religious rites and ceremonies.

Father Mike at this parish encouraged me to attend the 100 Man Retreat in Bend, OR, during summer 2007. I attended, and it was a conscious renewal of my spiritual (and

10

worldly) journey.

1.2 Monastery of the Risen Christ

This Monastery is Benedictine, and it is located in San Luis Obispo, CA.

- **Benedictine**: An order of monks (or nuns) that follow The Rule of St. Benedict (530 AD). They strive for Christian perfection in community, during prayer (Liturgical), while separated from worldly concerns.
- **Camoldese**: An order of monks (or nuns) that follow the Rule of St. Benedict (530 AD) as updated by St. Romuald (1027 AD). Named after the Holy Hermitage of Camoldi in the mountains of central Italy.
- **Monastery**: Residence occupied by monks or nuns, living in seclusion under religious vows.
- **Oblate**: A layperson dedicated to a monastic or religious life.

1.2.1 Christmas Party, 2013

The Monastery's Christmas Party for 2013 was held on December 16th. I talked with Mary Kay at the party, and she said, "You need to contact Debbie, as she wants to share some information about the May 7th, 2013, death of her 19-year-old daughter, Christine."

Then I explained how the death deeply grieved me. And that I drove from Orange County to San Luis Obispo, CA and made it in time for the *Rosary, Funeral Mass, and Burial*. I hugged each family member

11

and expressed my condolences. Throughout these services, I was in awe of the tremendous community turnout. During the burial service, four horses were led up, and each horse touched the casket with his nose. While the casket was lowered it into the grave, I tossed in a little dirt and a flower.

During the next month or so I began writing a poem to Christine using some of the words I whispered to Debbie at the funeral, my memories of Christine, some information in her obituary, and my imagination of her in heaven.

I wanted my feelings to be shared with the grieving family. I had the poem printed and laminated. Every time I was in San Luis Obispo, I would go to her gravesite, say a few prayers and leave a couple of laminated cards for those who were tending the grave. I also left a card in many RCC's for others to read and pray for Christine and her family.

During the Christmas Party, Mary Kay asked, "Have you made contact with Debbie or the family"?

My response was "No."

"You need to call Debbie. I will get you the number."

The next morning at the *7 am Mass* Debbie was in attendance. The instant I saw her, I knew it was in response to my grief. It was something I needed; I was not consciously praying for it to happen. It was a little glimpse of the eternal for me.

Debbie and I connected after *Mass* and shared a few of our grief stories, and she invited me to her home to see and discuss additional information about the death of her daughter.

1.2.2 Dreams and Abbot David, 2009

During an Oblate meeting at the Monastery in 2009, Abbot David was giving a talk about **Dreams** and their meanings. He mentioned that dreams occur and are usually remembered, just before a significant event in a person's life. For instance, making a life-changing decision, deciding on a course of study, planning a major vacation, etc. After the talk, he asked if anyone had a dream they wanted to share. Several did, but I was too shy to hold up my hand.

Afterward, I went to Abbot David and told him about my dream. The best I can recall, it was about comforting a distraught woman because of her husband's refusal to accept Jesus Christ. Since he didn't believe in God, he would have no part in seeking forgiveness. She didn't want him to die and end up in hell. I was trying to convince her that God would accept him into heaven regardless of his religious beliefs. If your husband has a good heart and cares for his neighbors, he is a candidate for heaven. So please do not worry about his fate.

Abbot David listened carefully to my dream and then said, "I think you were trying to offer the woman spiritual comfort. I also believe you would be a good candidate for my School for Spiritual Directors. Get the paperwork, start the process, as we only have two openings left."

I started school the following week

13

and quickly learned the real meaning of community. Forty students and ten instructors shared common meals, *Mass*, study periods, quite time, and evening prayer in the Benedictine manner for ten days at the Old Mission, Santa Barbara, CA. It was wonderful. Another little glimpse of the eternal for me.

1.2.3 Meeting Father Daniel, 2014

I was on a mission: drive from Santa Ana, CA to San Luis Obispo, CA, on a Thursday; arrange a meeting with my friends Debbie and her husband, meet with Fr. Russ, determine the status of the Monastery of the Risen Christ, and then return home on Sunday afternoon.

The drive was pleasant and exhilarating. There's something about feeling the road through the steering wheel, getting that flash of colors streaming in from Mother Nature, and knowing you are searching for the unknown. It is similar to the very beginning of a great expedition; one that quickens the pulse sharpens the senses, heightens expectations, as something will indeed be revealed.

I met with Debbie and her husband on Friday at 8 pm. We reviewed materials they had collected since the death of their daughter Christine. It was eye opening for me to realize how many hearts Christine had touched in her 19 years. I was consoled by their enthusiastic and frank responses, as they were quite willing to talk about their feelings. It was very good for me to see that they were finding joy in the in the process of moving on.

Saturday after the *7 am Mass*, I learned Fr. Russ was not available. So, I drove out to the Monastery. To my surprise, no one was there. Then I noticed a man in the back courtyard. I asked, "Do you know where Fr. Ray or Br. Michael are"?

"No. But I am waiting for Father Daniel."

Then I went down to the chapel area and started arranging my books in the Monastery's bookstore. As I was counting books and rearranging some in the trunk of my car, a monk walked up and introduced himself as Fr. Daniel, and he asked what was I doing in the bookstore? In the process of explaining my actions, I asked him to step into the chapel, and I pointed to Father Ray's Contributor's Plaque. "That is my name, six of my grandchildren, and two of my great grandchildren."

His face lit up, and he said; "Now I know who you are. You have been discussed many times with Fr. Ray."

I said my primary interest at the time was determining the status of re-starting the Monastery under the combined *Benedictine and Camaldolese Rule*. This rule is the way of life at the monastery as defined by St. Benedict and later updated by St. Romuald.

We sat down in the chapel, and he described what was happening, and thought it would be good for new Risen Christ Monastery and the monks at the Hermitage, near Big Sur, CA. After approval of their combined rule for operation, the Monastery will have three years to prove it is capable of sustaining itself. Then we talked about Fr. Daniel's priorities and funding requirements for the Monastery start-up.

The conversation moved to my involvement with the Monastery. In 2002 for some unknown reason, I became interested in reading the *Bible*. After many attempts to do *Bible study* at the Old Mission RCC in SLO, CA an office receptionist told me to find Br. Steve in a back office. I noticed a big man sitting behind a desk with a computer on it, and he was looking directly at me.

"Are you Brother Steve?"

"Yes."

"Is that title like Brother and Sister?"

He somewhat angrily responded,

"Have you ever heard of a monk"?

"Yes, I have."

"Well, I'm a monk." Then he told me that the Monastery had *Lectionary* (book of *Scripture* readings appointed for Christian or Judaic worship) studies on Thursday night at 7:30 pm. And I should join.

I started with the study group and continued with them for nine years. We studied the *Bible* for many years and continued with the lives, poetry, and writings of some doctors of the RCC and other spiritual writers.

That kind of angry monk, Br. Steve, became my Spiritual Director. I told him at one session that meeting him was one of the best things that had ever happened to me. I believe that he is a real biblical scholar.

Later, I became a Spiritual Director

16

following two years at the Abbot David
Geraets School for Spiritual Directors, held in
the Mission at Santa Barbara, CA.

Fr. Daniel then told me about his
relationship with the Monastery. He was a
friend of Abbott David's for many years. He
was in attendance at Father Steve's
Ordination at Our Lady of the Nativity RCC in
San Luis Obispo, CA. Bishop Richard,
Diocese of Monterey, CA, presided at the
Ordination. Also, Father Daniel has been Fr.
Steve's Spiritual Director for many years.

After our discussion, I drove Fr. Daniel
up to the main house. We laughed about my
earlier anxiety of trying to get some idea of
what was going on with the status of the
Monastery. Then Fr. Daniel appeared with all
of the answers to my questions.
Coincidence? No. It was another little
glimpse of the eternal.

On the drive back home, I was happy
about my trip accomplishments.

1.2.4 Old Mission San Luis Obispo

Junípero Serra in present-day San Luis
Obispo, CA founded this Mission in 1772. The
RCC today is a Procathedral (church used
temporarily as a cathedral) and a parish
church of the Diocese (many parishes) of
Monterey.

In January of 2002, I moved to San
Luis Obispo, CA, and rented an apartment
near the Old Mission. I began attending the
7 am *Mass* and developed a stronger desire
to read the Bible. Reading the Bible coupled
with studies at the Monastery of the Risen

Christ led to the publication of my first book, *A Little Bible Guide for Carly*, Jim Leonard, Copyright 2005, Trafford Publications.

I began working with various ministries at the church: youth confirmation, adult initiation, and others. These activities contributed to my desire to become a Eucharistic (server of communion) minister, altar server, and lector (reader of Scripture). All were accomplished and continued until I moved to Fullerton, CA in the spring of 2010.

During the winter/spring of 2006 - 2007, I supported the Youth Confirmation team. My support included preparing a 42-slide PowerPoint presentation covering the entire Bible. Source data: *The Catholic Youth Bible (CYB), Jesus of History/Christ of Faith, Written on Our Hearts, and A Little Bible Guide for Carly*.

One morning in the parish church, the assembly was singing "Holy, Holy, Holy..." during a 7 am Sunday Mass; I had the sensation that my entire family (living and dead) was gathered around me, and we were all singing. After completing the song, the sensation stopped and everything was back to normal. Later, telling Monsignor Steiger about the experience, he smiled and said, "And you were probably the loudest one."

I don't know what that experience was about, possibly another little glimpse of the eternal. It was a happy experience although somewhat alarming. At times I have tried to picture my family gathered for an event and joyfully singing like an event at a park for a family reunion. I do have a few of these happy memories, but singing in the church was different. I think it was a message directly from my heart. I believe it's best to continue singing, with my whole being, until the answer is revealed.

1.2.5 Old Mission Santa Barbara

Spanish Franciscans founded the Old Mission Santa Barbara on December 4, 1786, in the city of Santa Barbara, CA. It is the tenth Old Mission established in California. The mission is part of the Los Angeles archdiocese, and it includes a Cathedral with an RCC church.

In 2009, I attended a two-week retreat at the Mission Renewal Center. The retreat covered the first year of Abbot David Geraets School for Spiritual Directors. Forty students and ten instructors shared meals, daily Mass, study periods, quite time, and evening prayer in the Benedictine manner. At the end of this retreat, I had a better understanding of the Holy Spirit's action in my prayer life, my personal life, and my quest for seeking the center of my soul (my spiritual journey). It was another little glimpse of the eternal.

In the summer of 2010, I attended another two-week retreat at the Mission, completed the school, and received a Certificate in Spiritual Direction.

1.2.6 Old Mission San Miguel

Mission San Miguel Arcángel, a Spanish mission founded by the Franciscans near the present-day town of San Miguel, CA.

Established on July 25, 1797, and then dedicated to St. Michael the Archangel. Today the mission remains in use as a parish church of the Diocese of Monterey.

In the winter of 2003, before the December 22nd earthquake, I attended a two-day retreat for the RCIA team members. The retreat was conducted by the Benedictine Monastery of the Risen Christ, at the request of the San Luis Obispo Mission Church. During this retreat, I experienced some techniques for entering conscious union with Scripture. One technique is to select a passage or verse from the Bible and slowly read it several times. After a short period insert yourself into the scene and note your feelings and emotions.

Sitting in the courtyard of the Mission, I chose the passage with Zechariah and Gabriel in the Temple (Lk 1:5-25). Zechariah is performing his priestly service at the altar of incense in the Temple. Gabriel appears and announces the birth of a long-awaited son to be named John. Zechariah is fearful and doesn't readily accept the message because his wife Elizabeth is old and barren. Zechariah is made speechless and unable to talk until the message is fulfilled and the child (John the Baptist) is born.

Slowly and attentively reading this Scripture passage, I became another character in the scene. I was hidden from Zechariah's sight but was able to watch and hear the discourse about John. At some point, the smell of incense contributed to my awareness of being in the scene. It was another little glimpse of the eternal for me.

20

1.2.7 Old Mission San Antonio

Mission San Antonio de Padua founded by the Franciscans, near the present-day town of Jolon, CA. Established on July 14, 1771, and then dedicated to Saint Anthony of Padua. This mission is the third Mission founded in California by Father Junipero Serra. It was closed for six years following the San Simeon Earthquake in 2003. The mission reopened on September 29, 2009. The mission today is an RCC parish church in the Diocese of Monterey.

In the winter of 2003 before the earthquake, I attended a two-day retreat for the RCIA team members. The retreat was conducted by the Monastery of the Risen Christ, at the request of the San Luis Obispo Mission Church. My support for the team included providing some simple steps for conducting Lectio Divina, which is an ancient monastic prayer for continuously seeking God. This retreat was possibly another little glimpse of the eternal for me.

1.3 St. Joseph's Oratory of Mount Royal

St. Joseph's Oratory of Mount Royal is an RCC minor basilica (church with special ceremonial rights) and a national shrine on Westmount Summit in Montreal, Quebec. An Oratory is a structure, other than a parish church, used for prayer and the celebration of Mass. This Oratory is recognized as the largest shrine in the world dedicated to St. Joseph. Br. André and friends founded it in 1904. It has an outside garden displaying the 14 Stations of the Cross.

These stations are representations showing Christ carrying his cross to his crucifixion, death, and burial. In the RCC they are typically placed at intervals along the sidewalls of the church. St. Francis of Assisi began a tradition of moving from one station to the next in celebration of the Passion (to suffer) of Christ. It is observed during Lent, and especially on Good Friday. The Gospels (Matthew, Mark, Luke, and John) provide descriptions of Christ's Passion. The Passion is commemorated in Holy Week, from Palm Sunday and ending on Easter Saturday.

Whenever (1977 through 1986) I had consulting jobs in Montreal, I would always take the time to visit the church or attend Mass. On one occasion, I was exploring the Stations of the Cross statues positioned along a gravel path in an exterior garden. When I stopped to carefully observe the crucifixion station, I became mesmerized by the sight of Christ, and started crying, outwardly, and uncontrollably. I stepped back from the statue, composed myself, and walked away.

On the way to my car, I kept thinking about what had happened. To no avail, I couldn't explain it, nor find a cause. Getting into my car, I started crying again. Later, driving back to my hotel, I started crying for the third time. I pulled over to the curb and again composed myself. There must be something about the crucifixion of Jesus that I need to know. While in Montreal, I was not able to discern the cause of crying at the

22

sight of Jesus on the cross. It was another little glimpse of the eternal for me.

Years later I learned that the RCC doctrine, liturgy (collective formulas for the conduct of divine services), and celebration of the Mass are all in honor of Christ's self-sacrifice in accord with his Father's will.

1.4 The 100 Man Retreat

I attended this three-day retreat during the summer of 2007. The retreat was held at a campsite near Bend, OR. A Catholic group from New Mexico sponsored it. During the retreat, I experienced the solitude of a remote mountain setting, without the hectic cell phone, computer, television, traffic, etc. of the workplace. We were assigned cabins in groups of six, gathered together for meals, and common learning exercises. In the evenings we gathered outdoors around a large bonfire for singing and counseling.

My small group of six included a priest, banker, construction worker, dentist (from Canada), and one more. We met quietly during the day and shared our personal experiences. Some were struggling with past errors of judgment. Just quietly listening without comment, seemed very helpful. Getting away from the world, immersed in Creation, was a conscious renewal of my spiritual journey. It was also another little glimpse of the eternal for me.

The big event for me was a "spirit quest," which included taking a small backpack, a canteen of water, and then start walking into the mountains. Find a spot to sit and rest in a place where another person cannot be seen or heard. Draw a circle around the area using a stick or rock, then sit within the circle and stay there for three hours. During this time, listen attentively to the environment, and draw or write your perceptions.

My experience included hearing a loud crashing sound of something running through the forest. In a few minutes a large antlered buck stopped briefly to size me up, he was about 15 yards away from me and then continued in the forest. There is something about seeing wildlife up close and personal that stimulates my senses, making it a very pleasing and exhilarating experience.

This three-day event let each person live in the community, to see something other than self, and continue the inward journey to the Almighty Creator of heaven and earth. The event helped me to be aware of messages that come directly from my heart. The event was another little glimpse of the eternal for me.

APPENDIX A --- Acronyms

APPENDIX A --- Acronyms & Abbreviations			
Acronym	Meaning	Notes	Location
AD	Anno Domini	Latin for "In the year of our Lord"	2.1.6
BC	Before Christ	Date	
CRS	Catholic Relief Services	Christian Charity	2.5
CYB	Catholic Youth Bible	Bible	1.2.4, 1.2.7
ISBN	International Std Book No.	Front Matter	Front Matter
NRSV	New Revised Std.Version	of the Bible	Front Matter
OP	Order of Preachers	Dominican	2.1.5, 2.1.6
RCC	Roman Catholic Church		1.1 thru 1.4
RCIA	Christian Initiation of Adults	Catholic Rite	1.1.1, 1.2.6
SLO	San Luis Obispo	City & County in California	1.1.8, 1.2, 1.2.4

APPENDIX B --- Catholic Terms

Appendix B - Glossary of Catholic Terminology	
Term	**Meaning**
Abbess	Superior of a convent of nuns (women).
Abbott	Superior of a monastery of monks (men).
Absolution	Forgiveness of sins by a priest.
Adoration	Prayer Type: profess our love of God, acknowledging all the glory and wonder of God.
Anchoress	A woman who chooses to live a solitary life of prayer, withdrawn from the world.
Apostles	Twelve men selected by Jesus to witness His life, death, resurrection, and to preach the Gospel, and continue His mission in the world.
Archdiocese	The diocese of an archbishop, with several dioceses and parishes.
Baptism	The basis of Christian life, the sacrament of regeneration through water and in the Word of God.
Basilica	An RCC with special ceremonial rights.
Benedictine	An order of monks (or nuns) that follow The Rule of St. Benedict (530 AD). They strive for Christian perfection in their community, during prayer (Liturgical), while separated from worldly concerns.
Bible	The Bible (God's Word) is the sacred books of the Old and New Testaments.
Blessed	The consecrated Body and Blood

Appendix B - Glossary of Catholic Terminology	
Term	**Meaning**
Sacrament	of Christ (bread and wine).
Camaldolese	Monks and nuns that are part of the Benedictine family of monastic communities that follow the Rule of St. Benedict and St.Romuald. Named after the Holy Hermitage of Camoldi in the mountains of central Italy.
Canticle	One of the non-metrical hymns or chants from the Bible used in RCC services, or a song, a poem, or hymn of praise.
Carmelite Order	A major religious Order founded on Mount Carmel (Italy). It is a brotherhood of friars and cloistered nuns, and their charism (or spiritual focus) is contemplation.
Catechism	The Catechism of the RCC is used for teaching basic Christian truths. It is formulated to promote understanding, perception, and lively reception.
Cathedral	The central church of diocese (many parishes) that serves as the chair (authority) of its bishop.
Catholic	Relating to the RCC.
Centering Prayer	Silent prayer (an interior prayer) that prepares one to receive the gift of contemplative prayer. In this prayer, one can experience God's presence, closer than consciousness itself.
Charism	A divinely bestowed power (or talent), used to maintain spiritual

Appendix B - Glossary of Catholic Terminology	
Term	**Meaning**
	focus, during prayer and contemplation.
Communicant	A person who receives the Holy Eucharist (holy communion).
Communion	In a reenactment of the Last Supper, the words of Jesus -- "This is my body" and "This is my blood" -- are spoken over bread and wine by the priest and then shared by the worshipers.
Confession	Expression of sorrow and guilt for sinful thoughts or acts.
Confirmation	Seals a person with the gift of the Holy Spirit.
Contemplatio	A "movement" in Lectio Divina (Silently Listening, Quietly Resting in God).
Contemplation	The highest expression of man's intellectual and spiritual life, it is a period of resting in God.
Contrition	Detestation (hatred) of past sins and a resolve to make amends.
Convent	A society or association of monks, friars, or nuns: now usually used for nuns.
Creed	A statement of belief (faith) for use by Christian Catholics.
Diocese	A diocese consists of many parish churches.
Discalced	Barefooted: the term is used to denote friars and nuns who wear sandals.
Doctor	Individuals whom the Church recognizes as having been of particular importance, regarding

Appendix B - Glossary of Catholic Terminology

Term	Meaning
	their contribution to theology or doctrine.
Doctrine	A body or system of teachings by the Church.
Dominican Order	Order of Preachers (O.P.) is a major RCC religious order founded by the Spanish priest Saint Dominic de Guzman.
Eucharist	The consecrated elements of Holy Communion (bread and wine).
Foundress	A woman who establishes an institution or religious order.
Franciscan Order	A major religious order founded by St. Francis of Assisi in the 13th century. The order includes Friars Minor (men), the Order of St. Clare (women), and the Third Order of St. Francis (laypersons). They are members of mendicant friars or nuns (dependent on alms for sustenance).
Friars	Members of mendicant (beggars) religious orders of the RCC, Black Friars (Dominicans), Grey Friars (Franciscans), White Friars (Carmelites), etc.
Gospel	The heart of the sacred books for Christians because they are the principal source for the life and teachings of Jesus Christ. The term gospel refers to any of the first four books of the New Testament, namely Matthew, Mark, Luke, and John.
Habit	Attire of a religious order.

Appendix B - Glossary of Catholic Terminology

Term	Meaning
Hail Mary	Hail Mary full of Grace, the Lord is with thee. Blessed are thou among women and blessed is the fruit of thy womb Jesus. Holy Mary Mother of God, pray for us sinners now and at the hour of our death. Ref: www.catholicplanet.com/catholic/htm.
Homily	A sermon that normally follows the reading of the Gospel.
Incorrupt	Free from decay; fresh or untainted.
Intercession	Prayer Type: raise up the needs of others and our world.
Jesuits	The Society of Jesus is a global RCC male religious order founded in 1540 AD by Saint Ignatius of Loyola. His spiritual exercises help others to follow Jesus.
Jesus Prayer	Lord Jesus Christ, Son of God, have mercy on me a sinner, or Lord Jesus Christ, have mercy on us; or Jesus have mercy; or Jesus mercy; or Jesus.
Lectio	A "movement" in Lectio Divina (Reading Scripture with an Attentive Ear).
Lectio Divina	A Monastic practice of praying the Scriptures. During the prayer, the practitioner listens to the text of the Bible with the "ear of the heart," as if one is in conversation with God, and God is suggesting the topics for discussion.
Lectionary	A book of Scripture readings

Appendix B - Glossary of Catholic Terminology	
Term	**Meaning**
	appointed for Christian worship.
Lector	Reader of Scripture during a Catholic Mass.
Little way	St. Therese's "little way" of trusting in Jesus to make her holy and relying on small daily sacrifices instead of great deeds appealed to the thousands of Catholics and others who were trying to find holiness in ordinary lives. Ref: www.catholic.org/saints/saint.php?saint_id=105
Liturgy	The collective formulas for the conduct of divine services in Christian churches.
Mass	The celebration of the Eucharist that commemorates the death of Jesus. High Mass is celebrated according to the complete rite (the liturgy is sung by the celebrant). Low Mass (the liturgy is spoken not sung) and has a lesser ceremonial form than a High Mass, without music or choir.
Mendicant	Friars, monks, or nuns that are dependent on alms for sustenance.
Meditatio	A "movement" in Lectio Divina (reflecting on the meaning and message of Scripture).
Meditation	Meditation combines one's faculties of thought, imagination, emotion, and desire: to increase faith, to promote a conversion of heart, and to strengthen one's will

Appendix B - Glossary of Catholic Terminology

Term	Meaning
	to follow Christ.
Mental Prayer	Interior prayer or silent prayer.
Minister	Person authorized by the RCC to perform various functions in the church.
Monastery	Residence occupied by monks or nuns, living in seclusion under religious vows.
Monk	Many religious (monks, nuns, hermits) consecrate their lives to praise God and to intercede for His people.
Mystic	An individual who attains (or believes in achieving) insight into mysteries that transcend ordinary human knowledge.
Mystical	A means of having spiritual experiences that surpass natural human apprehension.
Mysticism	A system of contemplative prayer and spirituality aimed at achieving direct intuitive experience with the divine.
Nativity	An RCC festival that celebrates the birth of Jesus Christ; namely Christmas. The term as used herein is the name of a parish church.
Novena	An RCC ritual of the novena, wherein one repeatedly asks for the same favor over a period of nine days.
Nun	A woman that is part of a religious order, bound by vows of poverty,

Appendix B - Glossary of Catholic Terminology	
Term	**Meaning**
	chastity, and obedience.
Oblate	A layperson dedicated to a monastic or religious life.
Operatio	A "movement" in Lectio Divina (Our lived response to God).
Oratio	A "movement" in Lectio Divina (Praying in response to God's Word).
Oratory	A structure other than a parish church, set aside for prayer, the celebration of Mass, and other religious services.
Order	The major religious orders of the RCC (Franciscans, Benedictines, Dominicans, Carmelites, Trappists, etc.) have their own unique spirituality, their way of approaching God in prayer and living out the Gospel.
Ordination	Ordination in the RCC is the process by which male deacons and priests are consecrated (set apart) as clergy, for various religious rites and ceremonies.
Our Father	Our Father who art in heaven, hallowed be thy name, thy kingdom come, thy will be done on earth as it is in heaven, give us this day our daily bread, forgive us our trespasses as we forgive those who have trespassed against us, lead us not into temptation, but deliver us from evil. Ref: http://www.catholicplanet.com/catholic/our.htm

Appendix B - Glossary of Catholic Terminology

Term	Meaning
Paschal Mystery	The Paschal Mystery is one of the core doctrines of the RCC. It defines the heart of the Christian faith, namely the passion, death, and Resurrection of Jesus Christ.
Passion	The Passion ('to suffer') is the final short period in the life of Jesus that covers his visit to Jerusalem and his execution by crucifixion, an event central to RCC beliefs.
Penance	Penance is a sacrament of the RCC. It is a prayer of fasting as a voluntary self-punishment to atone for sins.
Petition	Prayer Type: ask for help or support for ourselves on our faith journey.
Poetry	Poetry in the Bible (Old and New Testaments) has been well defined as "the measured language of emotion."
Praise	Prayer Type: recognize all the goodness and wonder of God.
Priest	An ordained male member of the clergy of the order next below that of a bishop, and is authorized to carry out the Christian ministry.
Procathedral	A parish church used temporarily as a cathedral.
Psalms	A book of the Bible with a collection of 150 hymns, prayers, and songs that reveal all types of religious experiences. By fulfilling the Psalms, Jesus makes the Psalms His prayer book and that of

Appendix B - Glossary of Catholic Terminology

Term	Meaning
	the RCC for all time.
Purgatory	In the RCC, Purgatory is a place where souls of dying penitents (a person who confesses sin and submits to penance) are purified.
RCC	Roman Catholic Church
RCIA	The process of reconciling an adult into full communion with the RCC.
Rosary	The Rosary: a prayer of devotion to God by meditating on the lives of Jesus and Mary.
Sabbath	The Lord's Day. Christians keep Sunday as a weekly day of rest to commemorate the Resurrection of Jesus.
Sacrament	In the RCC the sacraments are baptism, penance, confirmation, the Eucharist, holy orders, matrimony, and anointing of the sick.
Sage	A wise person having wisdom, judgment, and experience.
Sanctity	Sanctity is holiness, saintliness, or godliness.
Scripture	Scripture refers to the sacred writings of the Old and New Testaments of the Bible.
Sonnet	Relatively short poems dealing with issues such as lost love.
Stigmata	Stigmata are markings on a persons body resembling the wounds of the crucified body of Christ.
Supplication	Prayer Type: ask God for something, for self or others

Appendix B - Glossary of Catholic Terminology

Term	Meaning
	(petitioning).
Tabernacle	A tabernacle is a solid, locked box in which, the Eucharist is "reserved" (stored).
Thanksgiving	Prayer Type: An expression of our gratitude for God's gifts in our lives.
Theatine	A priest of the Order of Clerks Regular.
Transformation	To become vessels [containers] of God´s compassionate love for others.
Trappist Order	Members of a brotherhood known for its modest lifestyle and vow of silence in which all conversation is forbidden.
Vatican II	The 2nd Vatican Ecumenical Council (1962 - 1965) of the RCC. Redefined the nature of the church. Increased lay participation in the liturgy.
Vespers	Vespers, an RCC service in the late afternoon or the evening.
Vessel	In the RCC, vessels are containers of God´s compassionate love for others.
Welcoming Prayer	A way of consenting to God's presence (and action) in one's physical and emotional reactions to events in daily life.

About the Author

Mr. Leonard is a devout Christian Catholic and an Oblate for the Benedictine Monastery of the Risen Christ in San Luis Obispo, CA. His spiritual path included in-depth Bible Study and study of mystic saints. Lectio Divina, centering prayer, and contemplative prayer furthered his desire to help others find their spiritual path. His recent catholic connections include:

- Procathedral San Luis Obispo (SLO), Old Mission, CA.
- Monastery of the Risen Christ, SLO, CA.
- St. Philip Benizi, Fullerton, CA.
- Holy Family Cathedral, Orange, CA.

Accomplishments at the Holy Family Cathedral include: attending daily Mass, daily communicant, and serving as a weekday lector.

His books include: "*A Little Bible Guide for Carly,*" Jim Leonard, Trafford Publications, 2005. "*Tears to Laughter,*" Debra Davis Hinkle and Jim Leonard, Dac Says Publishing, 2013.

He can be reached at jamesleonard08@gmail.com

www.ingramcontent.com/pod-product-compliance
Lightning Source LLC
Chambersburg PA
CBHW030309030426
42337CB00012B/649